The Passport Kids

Adventures in: Kraków, Poland

Written by: Ashlee Zora

To my three incredible kids—
You are my greatest adventure and the
reason I keep dreaming big. Watching you
explore the world with curiosity and
courage inspires me every day.
This book is just the beginning of sharing the
amazing journeys we've taken together.
I hope it reminds you of all the fun we've had
and the memories still waiting to be made.
Love always, Mom

The sun peeked through the clouds as Ella, Lucas, and Lily skipped
through the cobblestone streets of Kraków (KRAH-koof).
The city was buzzing with life—street performers played music in the square,
and the smell of freshly baked obwarzanki filled the air.

"I can't wait to try everything!" Ella grinned, rubbing her tummy.
"Pierogi, zapiekanki, pączki, lody... where should we start?"

Lily zipped past on her scooter. "No way, Ella! First, we're heading to
Wawel Castle. I heard there's a dragon!"

Lucas laughed, chasing after her.
"A dragon? Do you think it breathes fire?" with a grin.
"Anyways, I'm hungry, let's eat first!"

At the first food stand, Lily's eyes lit up.
"Pierogi!" she cheered, pointing to the
little dumplings filled with cheese and potatoes.
"Mmm," she said, taking a bite. "It's like a little pocket of yum!"
" Dziękuję" (jen-koo-yeh), Ella exclaimed,
saying thank you to the street vendor.

Ella's lips curled into a thoughtful smile.
'What about zapiekanki (zah-pye-KAN-kee)?
I'm in the mood for something new!"
They strolled to another cart where the vendor
handed them a long, toasted baguette.
Lucas took the first bite. "Whoa! It's like pizza... but on bread!"

At the edge of the square, Ella spotted a cart piled high with obwarzanki.
She dashed over, her mouth already watering.
"What's an ob-war-what?" Lucas asked, tilting his head.
"Obwarzanek Krakowski (ob-var-ZHA-neck kra-KOV-skee),"
Ella said slowly, like a teacher. "It's kind of like a bagel, but different.
The outside of the obwarzanek has a slight crunch and it's golden-brown,
like a yummy treasure! You can see it braided on top.
Inside, it's soft and fluffy, almost like a pillow! And they're soooo good."

She picked one covered in sesame seeds and took a big bite.
"See?" she said through a mouthful.
Lucas shrugged and grabbed one for himself.
"Not bad," he said with a grin.
Lily rolled her eyes. "Come on! We can't eat all day.
The dragon is waiting!"

The siblings raced along the path to Wawel (VAH-vel) Castle, Lily zipping
ahead on her scooter while Lucas and Ella hurried to keep up.
The castle towers rose high above them, like something out of a storybook.
"Do you think knights really lived here?"
Lucas asked, looking up at the stone towers.
"Probably," Lily said, "but I'm more excited about the dragon!"

At the base of the castle, the siblings found the legendary
Wawel Dragon statue, Smok Wawelski (smok vah–VEL–skee).
Just as they walked up, flames shot out of its mouth,
and Lucas jumped back in surprise.
"Whoa! Did you see that?" he shouted.
Lily laughed. "You almost dropped your obwarzanek!"
Ella snapped a photo of them in front of the dragon.
"Smile! This is one for the scrapbook."

After their dragon adventure, the siblings headed
back to Old Town for a treat. Lily's scooter wheels
squeaked as she came to a stop in front of a lody shop.
"Lody (LOH-dee)! Ice cream!" she shouted, hopping off.
"What flavor should we get?" Ella asked, scanning the colorful options.
Lucas held up a cone stacked with chocolate, vanilla, and strawberry scoops.
"All of them!" They found a spot by the fountain to sit and enjoy their lody.
"This," Ella said between bites, "is the best day ever."

"All aboard!" Lucas shouted as the train pulled into the station.
He and Lily scrambled to find a window seat while
Ella carefully carried a bag of obwarzanki for the ride.
"Are we almost there?" Lily asked, pressing her nose to the window.
"Not yet," Ella said, unwrapping another snack.
"But just wait until you see it. The rides, the games,
the water park... and don't forget the roller coasters!"

Lucas grinned. "I'm going to ride the biggest one."
Lily raised an eyebrow. "You mean the one that goes upside-down?
We'll see about that!"

The train clicked and clacked through the countryside,
and before they knew it, they arrived at the amusement park.

The siblings ran through the gates, their eyes wide as they took in the bright lights and towering rides.

"Let's start with the bumper cars!" Lucas shouted, dragging Lily and Ella behind him.

After a few rounds of bumping and laughing,
they moved on to the roller coaster.
As the car climbed higher and higher, Lucas held his breath.
"Not scared, are you?" Ella teased.
"Me? Never!" Lucas replied, gripping the bar tightly.

When the ride zoomed down, all three kids screamed
and laughed at the top of their lungs.
They stumbled off the ride, dizzy but happy.
They wrapped up their exciting day by splashing
down the twisty water slides and diving into the
sparkling pool, giggling as the cool water tickled their toes.
"This is the best day ever!" Lucas declared.

The next day, the siblings made their way to the Wieliczka Salt Mines.
"Cześć!" (cheshch), the siblings said hello to their guide.
"Wait... this whole place is made of salt?" Lucas asked, wide-eyed.
"Even the walls?!" Lily said, running her hand along the side.
"You can taste it if you–"
"Ew! Don't lick the wall!" Ella interrupted, laughing.
Their guide led them deeper into the mine, where the walls
glittered like they were sprinkled with tiny diamonds.

They entered a huge chamber filled with chandeliers
made of salt hanging from the ceiling.
"This is a chapel," the guide explained. "Carved entirely
from salt by miners hundreds of years ago."
"It's like a secret palace underground!"
Lily exclaimed, spinning around.

In another chamber, they found an
underground lake, so still it looked like glass.
"People used to float boats across it," their guide said.
"But now we just enjoy the view."
Lucas leaned over the edge. "Do you think there are fish down there?"
Ella pulled him back. "Don't fall in, Lucas! You'll turn into a salt statue!"

As they left the mines, Lily turned to the guide. "This was amazing!
I can't believe all of this is hidden underground!"
While walking back towards the mine's entrance,
their footsteps echoed softly against the salt walls.
They couldn't help but marvel at the incredible world
that had been carved deep beneath the earth.

They headed back to Kraków and walked through
Kraków's old town. Ella noticed some buildings looked very old.
"This city has a long and important history," their guide explained.
"During World War II, many people here suffered greatly.
But Kraków is also a city of hope and healing.

"People from all over the world now come to remember the past and celebrate how far we've come."
The siblings looked around with quiet respect, imagining the stories these ancient streets could tell.

They strolled through a neighborhood called
Kazimierz (kah-zhee-myezh), filled with
colorful buildings and lively cafes.
"This used to be a very special Jewish neighborhood,"
Ella read from her guidebook.
"For hundreds of years, Jewish families
lived, worked, and celebrated their culture here."

"During the war, many people were hurt, but
now the neighborhood remembers their
stories and keeps their memory alive."

Lucas looked thoughtful. "It's important to remember, right?"
"Yes," their guide smiled. "By remembering, we help make
sure something like that never happens again."

The next day, the siblings hopped off the bus in
Zakopane (zah–KOH–pah–neh), surrounded by towering mountains.
"Look at those peaks!" Lily said.
"I bet I can climb higher than you, Lucas."
"You wish!" Lucas raced toward a nearby trail.
The trail wound through tall pine trees, with crisp, fresh air.
Lucas and Lily raced ahead, hopping over rocks and roots.

At a clearing, they gasped.
Below them, a sparkling blue lake nestled
among green hills and jagged peaks,
called Morskie Oko, meaning 'Sea Eye'.
"It's like a postcard," Ella said softly.

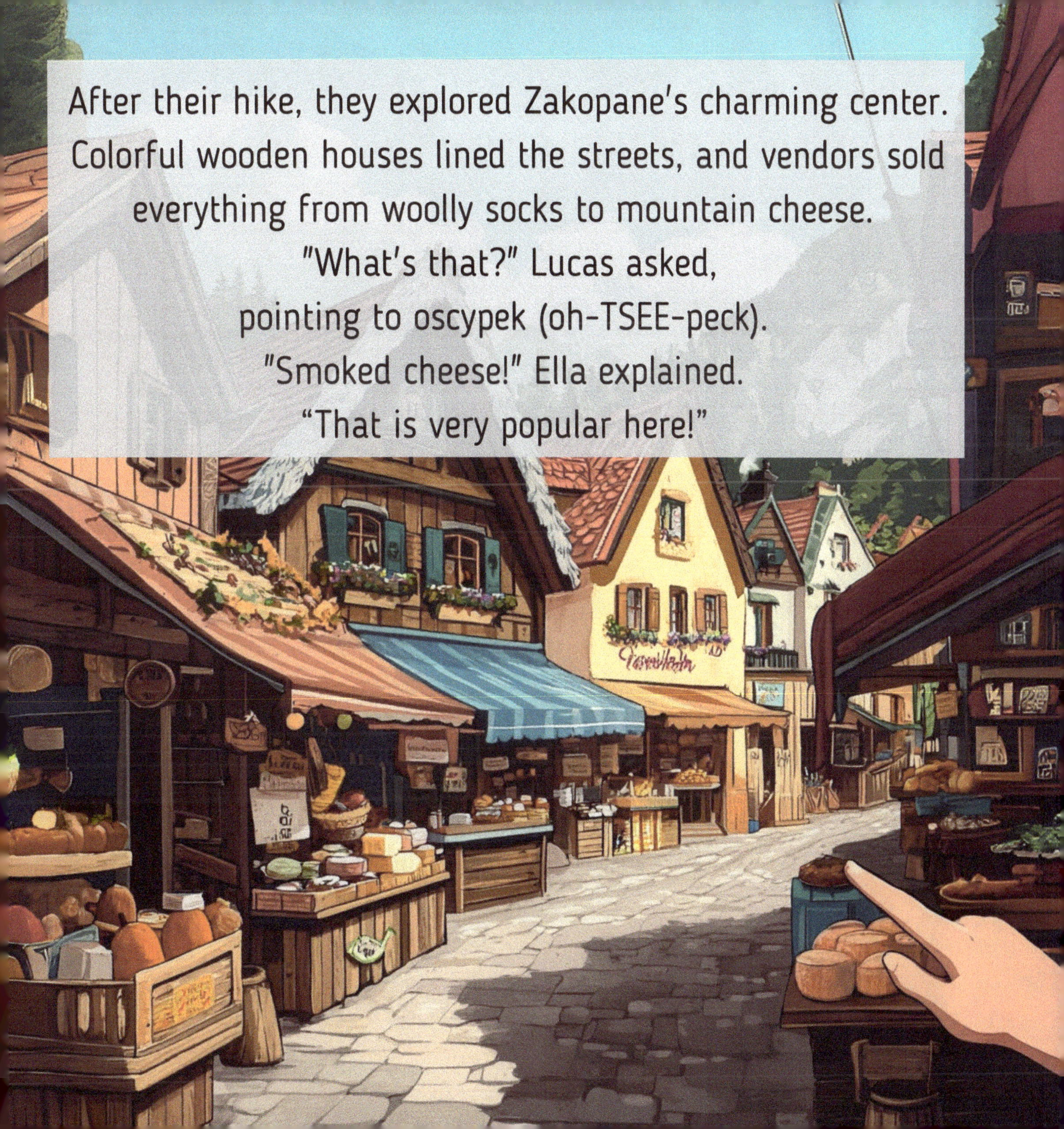

After their hike, they explored Zakopane's charming center.
Colorful wooden houses lined the streets, and vendors sold
everything from woolly socks to mountain cheese.
"What's that?" Lucas asked,
pointing to oscypek (oh-TSEE-peck).
"Smoked cheese!" Ella explained.
"That is very popular here!"

Later, they rode the Gubałówka (goo–BAH–woof–kah) gravity slide, racing down the mountain with wind rushing through their hair. "Wheeee!" Lily exclaimed! "I'm gonna win!" Ella shouted. "No way!" Lucas argued. As the sun set, painting the mountains pink and orange, Ella smiled. "This place is magical." As they made their way back into town, the siblings smiled at the memory of their adventure.

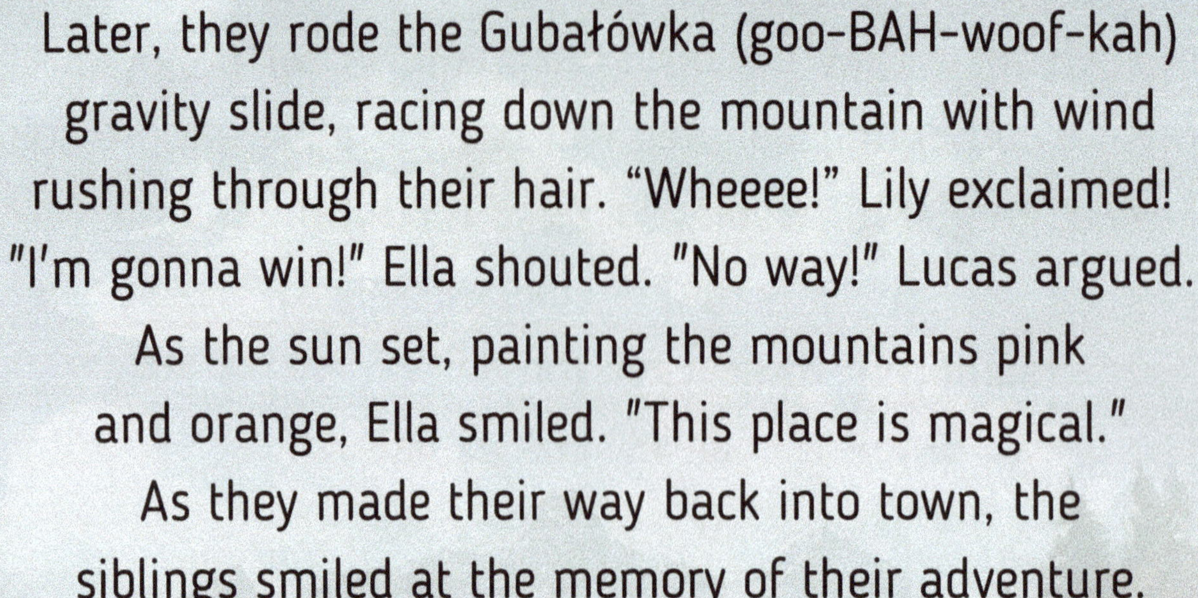

The bus ride back to Kraków was peaceful, the
siblings gazing out at the rolling countryside.
When they arrived in Old Town, the square buzzed
with life—vendors selling treats,
musicians playing melodies, and
families strolling under the twinkling lights.
"Before anything else, we need
pączki (POHNCH-kee)!" Lucas announced.

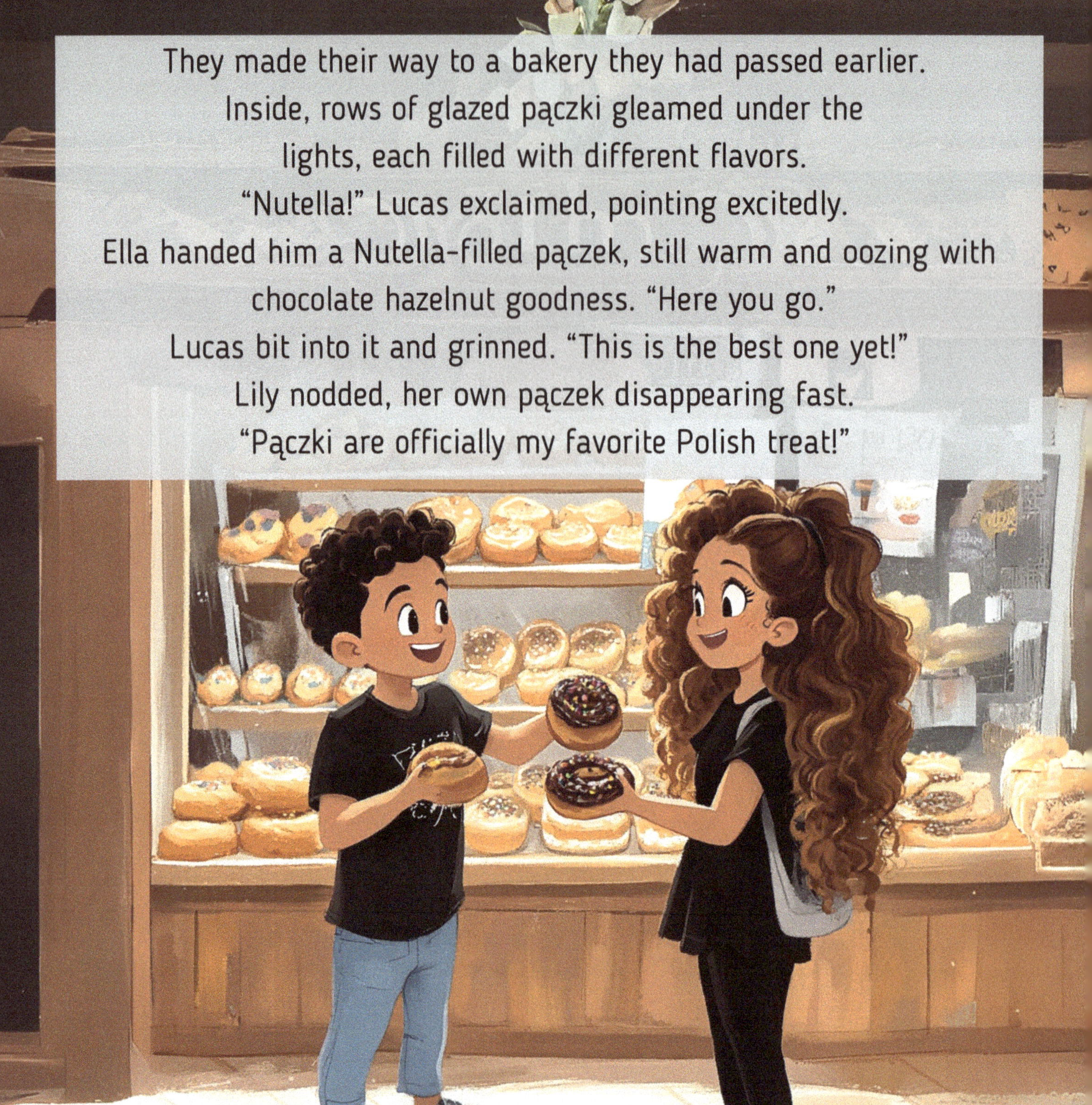

They made their way to a bakery they had passed earlier.
Inside, rows of glazed pączki gleamed under the
lights, each filled with different flavors.
"Nutella!" Lucas exclaimed, pointing excitedly.
Ella handed him a Nutella-filled pączek, still warm and oozing with
chocolate hazelnut goodness. "Here you go."
Lucas bit into it and grinned. "This is the best one yet!"
Lily nodded, her own pączek disappearing fast.
"Pączki are officially my favorite Polish treat!"

As night fell, the siblings wandered back into the main square.
A crowd had gathered in front of a tall tower,
where lights danced across the bricks.
"What's happening?" Lucas asked, squeezing
between people to get a better view.

Suddenly, music filled the air, and ballerinas
appeared—dancing on the side of the tower!

"They're flying!" Lily whispered in awe, her eyes wide.
"No, they're on wires," Ella corrected,
but her voice was just as amazed.
The ballerinas twirled and spun, their movements
perfectly timed with the music and the swirling lights.
The crowd cheered as the performance ended with
a grand finale—a burst of color lighting up the night sky.
"That was incredible," Lily said, clapping her hands.
"Poland is full of surprises," Ella agreed, smiling.

As they walked back toward their
apartment, the siblings passed a
violinist playing a soft tune under the stars.
Lily twirled in time with the music, Lucas took one
last bite of his pączek, and Ella carried their bag of treats.
"I love this city," Ella said.
"So do I," Lucas and Lily replied in unison.

On their way through the glowing streets of Kraków,
the sounds of music and laughter filled the air.
The siblings slowed their pace, savoring the moment.
"This has been the best trip ever," Lucas said, looking up at the stars.
"I don't want it to end," Lily added, skipping along the cobblestones.
Ella smiled. "It doesn't have to. We'll take all these
memories with us and maybe come back again someday."

They paused at the edge of the square, turning to take one last look at the bustling Old Town. The Wawel Castle towered in the distance, and the smell of fresh treats lingered in the air.

"Goodbye, Kraków," Lucas said softly.
"For now," Ella replied with a knowing grin.

Polish Words and Phrases

1. Cześć
- Pronunciation: "cheshch"
- Meaning: Hello or Hi.

2. Dziękuję
- Pronunciation: "jen-koo-yeh"
- Meaning: Thank you.

3. Kraków
- Pronunciation: "KRAH-koof" (Polish) or "KRAH-kov" (English)
- Meaning: A historic city in Poland, known for its medieval Old Town and cultural heritage.

4. Kazimierz
- Pronunciation: "Kah-zhee-myesh"
- Meaning: A historic district in Kraków, formerly the Jewish quarter, now a trendy area with cafes and galleries.

5. Oscypek
- Pronunciation: "oh-TSEE-peck"
- Meaning: A smoked cheese made from sheep's milk, traditional to the Tatra Mountains region.

6. Wawel
- Pronunciation: "VAH-vel"
- Meaning: The iconic castle and cathedral complex in Kraków, located on Wawel Hill.

7. Krakowski
- Pronunciation: "Krah-KOHV-skee"
- Meaning: Of Kraków or Kraków-style. Often used to describe local food, traditions, or designs.

Polish Words and Phrases

8. Pierogi (plural) , Pierog (singular)
- Pronunciation: "Pyeh-roh-ghee", "pye-roog"
- Meaning: Dumplings, typically filled with potato, cheese, meat, or fruit. A staple of Polish cuisine.

9. Zapiekanki (plural), zapiekanka (singular)
- Pronunciation: "Zah-pyeh-KAN-kee"
- Meaning: Open-faced baguettes topped with mushrooms, cheese, and other toppings, often called Polish pizza.

10. Obwarzanki (plural), Obwarzanek (singular)
- Pronunciation: "ob-var-ZHAn-Kee", "ob-var-ZHA-neck"
- Meaning: A circular bread, similar to a bagel, sprinkled with sesame seeds, poppy seeds, or salt. A popular Kraków street food.

11. Pączki (plural), pączek (singular)
- Pronunciation: "POHNCH-kee", "POHN-check"
- Meaning: Polish doughnuts, typically filled with jam, custard, or Nutella.

12. Lody (plural), lód (singular)
- Pronunciation: "LOH-dee", "lood"
- Meaning: Ice cream, beloved by locals and visitors in Kraków.

13. Zakopane
- Pronunciation: "Zah-KOH-pah-neh"
- Meaning: A mountain resort town in southern Poland, famous for its wooden architecture and outdoor activities.

14. Gubałówka
- Pronunciation: "Goo-BAH-woof-kah"
- Meaning: A mountain in Zakopane, accessible by funicular, offering scenic views and attractions like the gravity slide.